For my beautiful boys,
Jax and Jaid.
Without your love,
this book would
not be possible.
Mom (G.B)

I see you when I'm awake.
I hear you when I'm asleep.
I love you, Xavier.
Always.
Dad (S.A.J)

for
Jax and Jaid and Xavi

FIRST EDITION
10 9 8 7 6 5 4 3 2 1

Stranger Comics 4121 Redwood Ave, #101 Los Angeles, CA 90066

Printed in Honk Kong
100% Recycled Paper

Stranger Kids is a division
of Stranger Comics

strangerkids.com

Being born into a mixed race family is one
of the greatest gifts my parents gave me. While I
have not always known this to be true, as I have gotten
older I have come to know the importance of growing in an
environment where differences are applauded and individuality is a
goal to strive for. Today mixed race children must often search for
ways to have their identity affirmed and validated outside of their
family of origin, which can be a difficult journey. Reading imaginative and
creative bedtime stories like *I Am Mixed* celebrates our uniqueness while
defining what connects us one to the other. The good news is, the racial
barriers of yesterday are being shattered each and every day and mixed
race children are not only thriving but are emerging as some of the
most inspirational and dynamic leaders of the world.

*I Am Mixed is an invaluable
teaching tool that all children
of all races can learn from.*

~ Halle Berry

i am MIXED

written by

Garcelle Beauvais & Sebastian A. Jones

illustrated by

James C. Webster

art direction & storyboards
Darrell May

concept art
James C. Webster
Darrell May
Davida Benefield
Paul Davey

design & production art
Adrienne Sangastiano

editorial
Joshua Cozine

i am mixed like my twin brother Jay.

I am mixed with all kinds of goodies.

Like

Chocolate chunks and marshmallow delights,
candy canes with licorice stripes.

I am all things bright and soft and light.

And beautiful dark.

When I go to school I get asked funny things. **Like**

Your hair is bendy like curly wurly straws.
It's not straight like Sally's or thick like Lenore's.

I say
  I am all these things and so much more.

I am all things fine and fair and coarse.

And beautiful brown.

When I get home Mommy holds me high.
She says

*"Your skin is the night
and your eyes are the stars.
Your smile is the moon...*

i am mixed like my twin sister Nia.

I am mixed with all kinds of goodies.
Like

Vanilla beans and cinnamon sticks,
        rainbow sherbet with chocolate chips.

I am all things bright and soft and light.

And beautiful dark.

When I'm with family we play music.
Like

I sing
I am all these things and then some.

I am all things piano, bass and djembe drum.

And beautiful rhythm.

When I am finished dancing Daddy holds me high.
He says

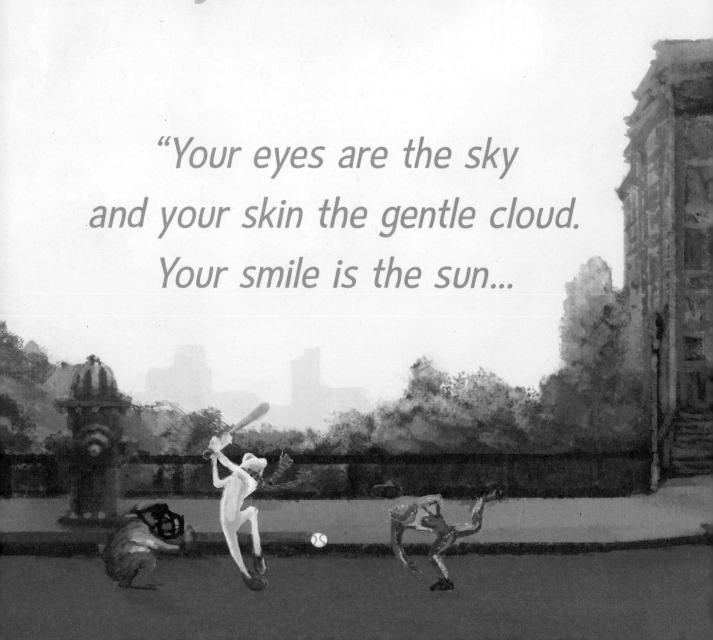

"Your eyes are the sky
and your skin the gentle cloud.
Your smile is the sun...

i am a melting pot of scrumptious treats.

i am an Irish jig to an African beat.

i am a Cuban painter with brush in hand.

i am a Haitian farmer healing the land.

i am a Chinese Dragon in search of Mars.

i am a Mexican sailor who travels afar.

i am the best from all over the world.

i am like every boy and every girl.

i am all these things like I've said before.

i am this and that and you know what's more...

Everyone in the world is a mix of two different families, but some people are lucky enough to be a mix of two different cultures. Being **mixed** can affect the languages you speak, the way you look, the traditions you have, and the things that are important to your family. Being **mixed** is just one way that you are extra special. So be proud of who you are and celebrate the things that make you YOU!

Love,

Grandpa

Grandpa

Grandma

Grandma

Mom

Dad

Brothers

Me

Sisters

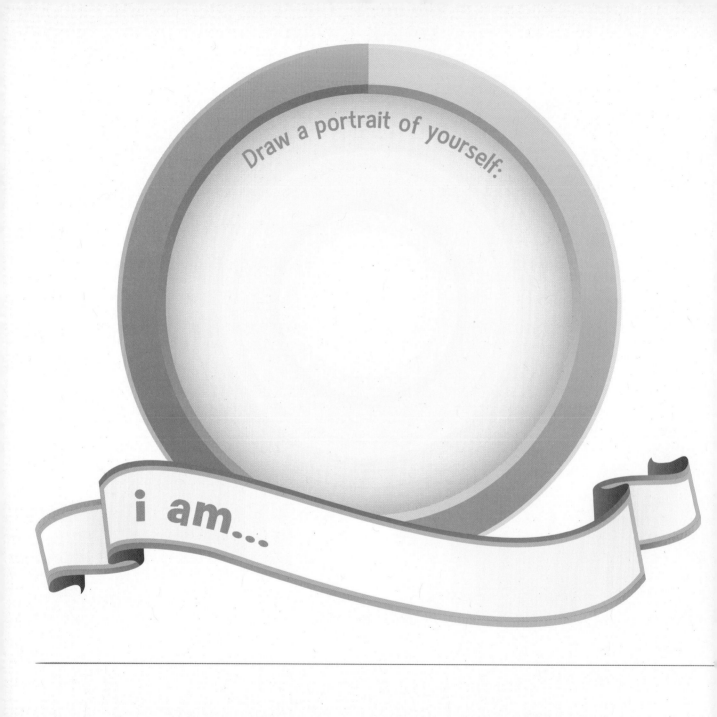

Draw a portrait of yourself:

i am...

about me...

My name is _____ .

I am _____ years old.

I have _____ brothers and _____ sisters.

My favorite color is _____ .

I was born in _____ .

My favorite song is _____ .

My favorite food is _____ .

My family speaks _____ .

My mom is from _____ .

My dad is from _____ .

This makes me special because _____

_____ !

A note for parents:

After sharing *I Am Mixed* with your child, you can use these discussion questions to help start a conversation about what it means to be mixed and why being mixed should be celebrated!

1. What does it mean to be mixed?

2. When Nia gets asked funny things at school, she doesn't get upset. She says "I am all these things and so much more." Why do you think she reacts this way? What does she mean?

3. Why do you think Jay's daddy is so proud of him?

4. What do Nia and Jay mean when they say "I am the best from all over the world. I am like every boy and every girl?"

5. In what ways are you mixed like Nia and Jay?

6. How will you celebrate being special, being mixed, and being YOU?

Meet the Pals

Prince Ranya III

I am a tree frog chief from the rainforest of Rio. I like to sing and dance and play games of chance.

Originally from England, **Sebastian** founded the critically acclaimed MVP records at 18, turning his love of American roots music into a business. More recently, he created Stranger Comics to do the same with his love of fanciful tales and quality escapism. Sebastian is honored to see the I Am Book Series come to life, celebrating the diverse mixed heritage he and his son share.

Stranger Comics
educational director
Megan Lewitin
marketing
Eddie DeAngelini
Hannibal Tabu
Tabitha Grace Smith
development
Mike Hodge
Christopher Garner
digital supervisor
Ken Locsmandi
art director
Darrell May
editor-in-chief
Joshua Cozine
publisher
Sebastian A. Jones

Born to create, **James** is a menagerie of artistic expression, interpretation and execution. Classically trained by an array of talented professors at Syracuse University, James has been working with the Stranger team since 2011. He currently resides in Atlanta with his extremely talented and brilliant lady, Adrienne, the designer and production artist for *I Am Mixed*.

Garcelle is Haitian born and immigrated to the United States at the age of seven. She has since charmed audiences with her dramatic and comedic abilities in both television and film. Always wanting to give back, Garcelle is active with charities including Step Up Women's Network, March of Dimes, and EDEYO, a Haitian children's organization. In addition to writing children's books, she has a popular monthly blog on People.com focusing on parenting and all things women. Garcelle lives in Los Angeles, where she is happiest spending time with her sons, Oliver and the twins, Jax and Jaid, who were the inspiration for the series.

We would like to thank

Paul Almond, TC Badalato, Marie Beaubien, Marie Claire Beauvais, Peter Bergting, Halle Berry, Andrew Cosby, Dawn Eyers, Mark Hovanec, Gray Jones, Lloyd Levin, Bob Lieberman, Lisa Ling, Laura Ling, Mona Loring, Andrew Matosich, Indira Salazar, Linda Salazar, Oliver Saunders, Shaun Shenassa, William Sobel, Dr. Sophy, Andrew Sugerman, Shel Talmy, Tim Taylor, Meghan Reynolds, Ron Richards, Elizabeth Ricin and David Uslan